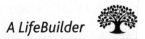

The CROSS

13 studies
for individuals or groups

John Stott

with Dale and Sandy Larsen

With Notes for Leaders

Scripture Union is an international Christian charity working with churches in more than 130 countries providing resources to bring the good news about Jesus Christ to children, young people and families – and to encourage them to develop spiritually through the Bible and prayer. As well as coordinating a network of volunteers, staff and associates who run holidays, church-based events and school Christian groups, Scripture Union produces a wide range of publications and supports those who use their resources through training programmes.

Scripture Union, 207–209 Queensway, Bletchley, MK2 2EB, UK.
e-mail: info@scriptureunion.org.uk
www.scriptureunion.org.uk

Scripture Union Australia: Locked Bag 2, Central Coast Business Centre, NSW 2252.
www.su.org.au

ISBN 978 1 84427 688 2

First published in the United States by InterVarsity Press 2009.
Published in Great Britain by Scripture Union 2012.

British Library Cataloguing-in-Publication data: a catalogue record for this book is available from the British Library.

In addition to *The Cross of Christ* (Downers Grove, Ill.: InterVarsity Press, 2006), this study adapts material from two other books by John Stott: *The Message of Romans, The Bible Speaks Today* (Downers Grove, Ill.: InterVarsity Press, 1994) in the Leader's Notes for studies four, five and twelve; and *The Message of Galatians, The Bible Speaks Today* (Downers Grove, Ill.: InterVarsity Press, 1968) in the Leader's Notes for study five.

Printed in India by Thomson Press India Ltd.

Contents

Getting the Most Out of
The Cross

Every religion and ideology has a visual symbol that illustrates a significant feature of its history or beliefs. The lotus flower, though used by the ancient Chinese, Egyptians and Indians, is now particularly associated with Buddhism. Ancient Judaism avoided visual signs and symbols for fear of infringing on the second commandment, but modern Judaism has adopted the Shield or Star of David. Islam is symbolized by a crescent, at least in West Asia, originally depicting a phase of the moon.

The secular ideologies of the twentieth century also have their universally recognizable signs. The Marxist hammer and sickle represent industry and agriculture. The swastika was adopted by some German groups as a symbol of the Aryan race; then Hitler took it over, and it became the sinister sign of Nazi racial bigotry.

Christianity is no exception in having a visual symbol. A universally acceptable Christian emblem would obviously need to speak of Jesus Christ, but there is a wide range of possibilities that could have been used. Christians might have chosen the manger in which the baby Jesus was laid, or the carpenter's bench at which he worked as a young man in Nazareth, or the boat from which he taught the crowds in Galilee, or the apron he wore when washing the apostles' feet, or the stone that was rolled away from the mouth of his tomb, or a throne symbolizing divine sovereignty, or a dove symbolic of the Holy Spirit sent from heaven on the Day of Pentecost. Any of these would have been suitable as a pointer to some aspect of the ministry of the Lord.

But instead, the chosen symbol came to be a simple cross. The early Christians wished to commemorate as central to their understanding of Jesus neither his birth nor his youth, neither his teaching nor his service, neither his resurrection nor his reign, nor his gift of the Spirit, but his death, his crucifixion.

No theology is genuinely Christian that does not arise from and focus on the cross. The cross is at the center of the historic biblical faith, and the fact that this is not always everywhere acknowledged is sufficient justification for preserving a distinctive evangelical testimony. Evangelical Christians believe that in and through Christ crucified, God substituted himself for us and bore our sins, dying in our place the death we deserved to die, in order that we might be restored to his favor and adopted into his family.

This is not a study on the atonement only, but on the cross. After three introductory studies, we come to the heart of the cross, looking at *forgiveness of sin* and emphasizing a truly biblical understanding of the notions of *satisfaction* and *substitution*. Then we move on to the three great achievements of the cross: *saving sinners, revealing God* and *conquering evil*. The final four studies grapple with areas often omitted from books on the cross: what it means for the Christian community to *live under the cross*. The cross transforms everything. It gives us a new worshiping relationship to God, a new incentive to give ourselves in mission, a new love for our enemies and a new courage to face the perplexities of suffering.

In daring to write (or read) a book about the cross, there is a great danger of presumption. What actually happened when "God was reconciling the world to himself in Christ" is a mystery whose depths we shall spend eternity plumbing. In addition, it would be most unseemly to feign a cool detachment as we contemplate Christ's cross. We are involved. Our sins put him there. Far from offering us flattery, the cross undermines our self-righteousness. We can stand before it only with a bowed head and a broken spirit. And there we remain until the Lord Jesus speaks to our hearts his word of pardon and acceptance, and we, gripped by his love and full of thanksgiving, go out into the world to live our lives in his service.

Suggestions for Individual Study

1. As you begin each study, pray that God will speak to you through his Word.

2. Read the introduction to the study and respond to the personal reflection question or exercise. This is designed to help you focus on God and on the theme of the study.

3. Each study deals with a particular passage so that you can delve into the author's meaning in that context. Read and reread the passage to be studied. The questions are written using the language of the New International Version, so you may wish to use that version of the Bible. The New Revised Standard Version is also recommended.

4. This is an inductive Bible study, designed to help you discover for yourself what Scripture is saying. The study includes three types of questions. *Observation* questions ask about the basic facts: who, what, when, where and how. *Interpretation* questions delve into the meaning of the passage. *Application* questions help you discover the implications of the text for growing in Christ. These three keys unlock the treasures of Scripture.

Write your answers to the questions in the spaces provided or in a personal journal. Writing can bring clarity and deeper understanding of yourself and of God's Word.

5. It might be good to have a Bible dictionary handy. Use it to look up any unfamiliar words, names or places.

6. Use the prayer suggestion to guide you in thanking God for what you have learned and to pray about the applications that have come to mind.

7. You may want to go on to the suggestion under "Now or Later," or you may want to use that idea for your next study.

Suggestions for Members of a Group Study

1. Come to the study prepared. Follow the suggestions for individual study mentioned above. You will find that careful preparation will greatly enrich your time spent in group discussion.

2. Be willing to participate in the discussion. The leader of your group will not be lecturing. Instead, he or she will be encouraging the members of the group to discuss what they have learned. The leader will be asking the questions that are found in this guide.

3. Stick to the topic being discussed. Your answers should be based on the verses which are the focus of the discussion and not on outside authorities such as commentaries or speakers. These studies focus on a particular passage of Scripture. Only rarely should you refer to other portions of the Bible. This allows for everyone to participate in in-depth study on equal ground.

4. Be sensitive to the other members of the group. Listen attentively when they describe what they have learned. You may be surprised by their insights! Each question assumes a variety of answers. Many questions do not have "right" answers, particularly questions that aim at meaning or application. Instead the questions push us to explore the passage more thoroughly.

When possible, link what you say to the comments of others. Also, be affirming whenever you can. This will encourage some of the more hesitant members of the group to participate.

5. Be careful not to dominate the discussion. We are sometimes so eager to express our thoughts that we leave too little opportunity for others to respond. By all means participate! But allow others to also.

6. Expect God to teach you through the passage being discussed and through the other members of the group. Pray that you will have an enjoyable and profitable time together, but also that as a result of the study you will find ways that you can take action individually and/or as a group.

7. Remember that anything said in the group is considered confidential and should not be discussed outside the group unless specific permission is given to do so.

8. If you are the group leader, you will find additional suggestions at the back of the guide.

1

The Centrality of the Cross

Isaiah 53

From Jesus' youth, indeed even from his birth, the cross cast its shadow ahead of him. His death was central to his mission. The church has always recognized this truth. The fact that the cross became the Christian symbol and that Christians stubbornly refused, in spite of ridicule, to discard it in favor of something less offensive can have only one explanation. It means that the centrality of the cross originated in the mind of Jesus himself. It was out of loyalty to him and the suffering he experienced that his followers clung so doggedly to this sign. It is our greatest comfort when we face our own times of difficulty.

GROUP DISCUSSION. People often say "If I'd only known . . ." Think of a time when you went through great difficulties. If you had known in advance how bad things would be, would you have gone through with it (assuming you had a choice)? Explain why or why not.

PERSONAL REFLECTION. When has a seemingly bad time turned out for your good or the good of others you know?

Jesus knew that he was going to die, not in the sense that all of us know we will have to die one day, but in the sense that he would meet a violent, premature yet purposeful death. From Isaiah 53 Jesus seems to have derived the clearest forecast not only of his sufferings but also of his subsequent glory. From this chapter more than any other he learned that the vocation of the Messiah was to suffer and die for human sin, and in so doing, be glorified. The person portrayed in these verses is commonly referred to as the Servant from the preceding portion of Isaiah (Isaiah 52:13). *Read Isaiah 53.*

1. What would you say is the central experience of the Servant in this passage?

2. How does the Servant presented here compare with the person you envision when you think of Jesus Christ?

3. The writer seems to assume that the message of these words will not be believed (v. 1). What would make this image of Christ unexpected and difficult to believe?

4. How is the Servant at odds with prevailing ideas of personal power (vv. 2-3)?

5. What purposes are fulfilled by the Servant's suffering (vv. 4-6)?

6. What various words does Isaiah use to describe those who benefit from the Servant's suffering (vv. 4-6)?

Isaiah repeatedly uses the pronouns *we, our* and *us* (vv. 2-6). How do you see yourself in this Scripture passage?

7. How does Isaiah change the sheep metaphor between verse 6 and verse 7?

8. What is unjust about the Servant's fate?

9. The mood of Isaiah's writing changes in verses 10-12. Question 5 looked at the purposes that were fulfilled by the suffering of the Servant. How do verses 10-12 expand on those purposes?

10. How will the Servant be vindicated at last?

11. We cling to the work of the cross as the center of our faith. What do you think most people consider the heart of Christianity?

12. How does the cross give you comfort in times of difficulty?

13. Spend a few minutes in quiet, reflecting on the cross of Christ and this study. How has this study challenged or confirmed your opinion about the heart of Christianity?

Thank Christ, the Suffering Servant, for humbling himself and bearing your sin.

Now or Later

Divide the group into two parts and read Isaiah 53 responsively. You may read alternating verses or divide each verse into two parts.

Ask people both in and outside your church fellowship this question: "What would you say is the heart of Christianity?" Compile answers and bring them next week. Note how frequently (or infrequently) people answer "the cross of Christ" or something similar.

2

Why Did
Christ Die?

Matthew 27:11-26

In any trial by jury, prosecutors and defense attorneys question prospective jurors closely. The lawyers know that each person, no matter how good a citizen, will come into the trial biased in certain ways. Some who are summoned for jury duty will have already made up their mind before they hear any evidence. Counsels for the prosecution and defense hope to exclude jurors who seem predisposed to vote against their clients, and they hope to keep those who seem sympathetic to their clients. One attorney or the other may have an uphill battle to win certain jurors over. When Jesus was brought to trial, there was no possibility of a just verdict. Everyone's mind was made up in advance. Everyone involved was predisposed to find him guilty.

GROUP DISCUSSION. Think of the three moral failings of *greed, envy* and *cowardice.* In your opinion, which is the most destructive, and why?

PERSONAL REFLECTION. Think of a time when you had to make a hard decision, one in which you were influenced both ways by different factors. Why and how did you choose the way you did? Do you think now that it was the right decision? Why or why not?

While the Roman procurator, Pilate, was convinced of Jesus' innocence, he made ingenious attempts to avoid having to come down clearly on one side or the other. Pilate wanted to avoid sentencing Jesus (since he believed he was innocent) and at the same time avoid exonerating him (since the Jewish leaders believed he was guilty). How could he contrive to reconcile these irreconcilables? We watch him wriggling as he attempts to release Jesus and pacify the Jews, that is, to be just and unjust simultaneously. *Read Matthew 27:11-26.*

1. While Pilate has Jesus in custody, he has several opportunities to let him go free. What are those occasions, and what does Pilate decide at each point?

2. Based on what you read here, how would you describe Pilate's character?

3. What fears does Pilate display?

4. Pilate asks "What shall I do, then, with Jesus who is called Christ?" (v. 22). How do his attempts to avoid responsibility in Jesus' trial parallel ways that people try to avoid submitting to Christ as Lord?

5. Pilate detects *envy* as the true motivation for the Jewish leaders' hostility to Jesus (v. 18). For what reasons might they be envious of Jesus?

6. When have you found the authority of Jesus in conflict with your own authority? Think especially of times when you have been called to inconvenient obedience.

7. What is Pilate trying to accomplish by his display of washing his hands (v. 24)?

8. In verse 25 Matthew writes that "all the people" said to Pilate, "Let his blood be on us and on our children." What do you think made them respond so forcefully here, when it seems they were undecided about Jesus just minutes before (see v. 20)?

9. Although Jesus is brought to his death by human sins, he does not die as a martyr. On the contrary, he goes to the cross voluntarily, even deliberately. In what sense has all of humanity done what the crowd did (in demanding that he be crucified) and what Pilate did (in actually "[handing] him over to be crucified")?

10. Before we can begin to see the cross as something done *for* us (leading us to faith and worship), we have to see it as something done *by* us (leading us to repentance). How do you respond to the idea that Jesus' crucifixion was done *by* as well as *for* humanity?

11. How do you respond to the idea that Jesus' crucifixion was done *by* you personally as well as *for* you personally?

---

12. Spend a few minutes in quiet reflecting on the cross and this study. How have your ideas been challenged or confirmed about why Christ died?

The cross is an exposure of human evil, but at the same time it is a revelation of the divine purpose to overcome the human evil thus exposed. Pray for deeper understanding and gratitude for Jesus' willingness to endure the cross for your sake.

Now or Later

Make a timeline of your own spiritual life. Using symbols, different colors, words or other indicators, show how your understanding of the cross of Christ has grown and developed and perhaps even gone through major changes at points of crisis.

Make a cross out of cardboard or wood. Have a time of prayer and confession in which you confidentially write your sins on slips of paper. Fold the papers so they cannot be read. Thumbtack them to the cross to symbolize (1) that your sins sent Jesus to the cross and (2) that he bore your sins there. Destroy the papers later so they cannot be read by others.

As preparation for the next study, read about the origins of the Passover in Exodus 11—12.

3

Looking Below
the Surface

Mark 14:12-26

We all have ways of remembering friends and family members who've died. We may visit their gravestone periodically. Most likely we have pictures of them on our walls or preserved in albums. We may tell favorite stories about them, or even write letters to them when we especially miss their presence in our life. We create significant ways of remembering that fit the person who's died.

When Jesus knew that he was about to die, he gave instructions ahead of time to his disciples for how they should remember him: through a living memorial we still practice today in honor of him.

GROUP DISCUSSION. Imagine that you are giving instructions that are to be shared at your own memorial service for some type of regular observance for people to engage in to remember you after your death. What would you ask people to do regularly in your memory? Why would you choose those particular activities?

PERSONAL REFLECTION. When has taking Communion been especially moving or meaningful to you? What makes those times stand out in your memory?

Our story begins on Maundy Thursday (the Thursday before Good Friday). Jesus had already seen the sun set for the last time. Within about fifteen hours his limbs would be stretched out on the cross. Within twenty-four hours he would be both dead and buried. And he knew it. Yet extraordinarily, he was thinking of his mission as still future, not past. He did not regard the death he was about to die as bringing his mission to an untimely end, but as actually necessary to accomplish it. The mission of a lifetime, the culmination of thirty to thirty-five years, was to be accomplished in its last twenty-four hours, indeed, in its last six. *Read Mark 14:12-26.*

1. Jesus' death is fast approaching. How do Jesus' words and actions in this passage compare to the words and actions of others you've known when they've been near death?

2. Jesus is spending his last evening on earth in quiet seclusion with his disciples. It is the first day of the Feast of Unleavened Bread and they meet to eat the Passover meal together. Usually it's a celebratory occasion for the Jews recalling their release from slavery in Egypt. We can picture them around a low meal-table, reclining on cushions on the floor. Jesus announces that one of them will betray him (vv. 17-21). All of them respond "Surely not I?" Why do you think each of them even entertains the possibility that they will be the one to betray Jesus?

3. How do people still betray Jesus today?

4. How do you think the disciples react to the startling words and actions that Jesus introduces into the Passover meal (vv. 22-25)?

5. Jesus identifies the bread as "my body" (v. 22). We should picture unleavened Passover matzo rather than familiar loaves of yeast bread. What is symbolic about what he does with the bread?

6. Jesus identifies the wine as "my blood of the covenant." What is symbolic about what he does with the wine (vv. 23-25)?

7. What do the disciples do with the bread and wine Jesus offers them (vv. 22-23)?

8. By the time the disciples sing a traditional Passover hymn and go out into the darkness, there are only eleven of them; Judas has left. What thoughts do you think fill their minds as they follow Jesus to the Mount of Olives (v. 26)?

9. Based on this Scripture passage, what purposes of God are fulfilled in the crucifixion of Christ?

10. What were your earliest ideas of the Lord's Supper, and how have they changed over the years?

---

11. The next time you take Communion, what do you think will be especially striking to you?

---

12. Spend a few minutes in quiet, reflecting on Jesus' last meal with his disciples before he was crucified. How does this lesson change or reinforce your understanding of Jesus?

Praise God that nothing can hinder his purposes. Thank him for his salvation through the broken body and poured-out blood of Jesus.

Now or Later

If it is suitable with the beliefs of all group members, have a Communion service together.

Discuss various ways that you have seen the Lord's Supper celebrated. Talk in positive terms about how each method affirms the purposes of God in the death of Christ.

Study 1 Corinthians 11:17-34 concerning the Lord's Supper.

4

The Problem of Forgiveness

Romans 2:1-11

Many people are bewildered by Christians' insistence that, according to the gospel, the cross of Christ is the only ground on which God forgives sins. Why does God not simply forgive us without the necessity of the cross? Nobody's death is necessary before we forgive each other. It sounds like a primitive superstition that modern people should have long since discarded.

The reason why many people give the wrong answers to questions about the cross, and even ask the wrong questions, is that they have not carefully considered the seriousness of sin or the majesty of God.

GROUP DISCUSSION. What do you think of when you see or hear the word *sin?*

PERSONAL REFLECTION. Do you think the concept of sin is overemphasized or underemphasized today?

What changes do you think would be healthy in the way people think of sin?

In Romans 1:18—3:20, the apostle Paul demonstrates the universality of human sin by dividing humanity into three sections and accusing them one by one: depraved Gentile society (1:18-32); critical moralizers, whether Gentiles or Jews (2:1-16); and well-instructed, self-confident Jews (2:17—3:8). He then concludes by accusing the whole human race (3:9-20). *Read Romans 2:1-11.*

1. According to this passage what is so bad about self-righteousness?

2. Where do you see yourself in this passage? (If you don't see yourself in this passage, why do you feel that it doesn't apply to you?)

3. What is your reaction to the prominence of God's wrath and judgment in this passage?

4. How does Paul demonstrate that no one is immune from God's judgment (vv. 1-4)?

5. What characteristics of God balance the judgment of God in verse 4?

6. Consider your own experience of coming to faith in Christ. How did God's kindness lead you to repentance? How does God's kindness continue to lead you to repentance?

---

7. What warnings for the self-righteous do verses 4-5 contain?

---

8. Why is God's holiness incompatible with human rebellion against God?

---

9. What does the future hold for those who do evil (vv. 6, 8-9)?

---

10. What does the future hold for those who do good (vv. 6-7, 10)?

---

11. If Romans 2:1-11 was all you knew of Scripture, how would you size up your condition, including your hope for the future?

12. In light of our studies so far and your own understanding, how does the cross of Christ reconcile the holiness of God and the love of God?

---

13. Spend a few minutes in quiet, reflecting on the cross and the problem of forgiveness. How have your ideas been challenged or confirmed about the nature of God's forgiveness?

Thank God for his holy love, which takes sin seriously and still yearns over sinners. Personally thank him for respecting you enough to take your own sin seriously yet yearning over you enough to provide a way for you to be forgiven.

Now or Later

Reread Romans 2:1-3 slowly. Is your conscience nudged about someone you look down on or tend to judge? Write two prayers: a prayer confessing self-righteousness and a prayer asking God to bless and help that person.

Consider this statement: "We learn to appreciate the access to God, which Christ has won for us, only after we have first seen God's inaccessibility to sinners. We can cry *Hallelujah* with authenticity only after we have first cried *Woe is me, for I am lost.*" If this is true, what are the implications for public and private worship?

5

Satisfaction for Sin

At some time or another, we all face situations that don't have an easy solution. People in positions of leadership, especially, are frequently called on to make decisions that affect many people. Whether it's teaming up with coworkers to devise more efficient ways to accomplish tasks, or making decisions that restore peace and deepen communication in our homes, it takes wisdom and work to reach a solution that satisfies everyone.

After the Fall, God faced what looked like an impossible problem: how to reconcile his holy love—a love that abhors sin and can't touch it—with his deep love for us and his desire to be in relationship with us.

GROUP DISCUSSION. What's the most difficult problem you've had to solve? How did you come up with a solution? Did it satisfy everyone?

PERSONAL REFLECTION. How has God shown himself to be consistent and unchanging in your life?

The essential background to the cross is a balanced understanding of the gravity of sin and the majesty of God. If we diminish either, we diminish the cross. If we reinterpret sin as only a lapse instead of a rebellion, and God as indulgent instead of indignant, then the cross appears superfluous. Furthermore, those reinterpretations degrade both God and humanity. A biblical view of our sin and of God's wrath honors both. It honors humans by affirming them as responsible for their actions. It honors God by affirming him as having moral character.

In the previous study we saw how Paul established our hopeless condition before God. God is holy and just; we are sinful and under his judgment. However, Paul's analysis of our condition is not the end of his argument. *Read Romans 3:19-26.*

1. In one sentence how would you state the good news of this passage?

2. Which part of this passage brings you the most hope, and why?

3. How does this passage contradict human pride?

4. "The law" (vv. 19-20) is God's law revealed in the Old Testament. What does the law accomplish for us?

5. God is both the Judge who must punish evildoers and the Lover who must find a way to forgive them. In verses 21-24 how are God's judgment and God's love reconciled?

6. What is the significance of the phrase "apart from law" (v. 21)?

7. Paul twice refers to "righteousness from God" (vv. 21-22). How does he expand on this phrase (vv. 21-24)?

8. What does the phrase "a sacrifice of atonement" mean (v. 25)?

9. Paul twice says that Christ's death demonstrates God's justice (vv. 25-26). How would you explain his repeated statement?

10. What are some other ways, besides faith in Jesus, that people imagine they can satisfy God's righteous requirements?

11. Which of these inadequate means of satisfying God have been most tempting to you?

12. Spend a few minutes in quiet. How has this study affected your ideas about sin and God's righteousness?

Praise God for taking the initiative to do something about our rebellion against him, not leaving us to go our own way.

Now or Later

Expand on questions 10-11 by naming all the inadequate ways you can think of by which people try to satisfy God's requirements. Explore how each method appeals to human self-sufficiency and pride. Consider how these false ways could even show up in the life of a church.

Looking toward the next study, study Leviticus 16 concerning the Old Testament sacrifices for the Day of Atonement.

6

Ransomed by God

As a child did you ever pay a sibling or other family member to do an unpleasant chore for you? Were you ever on the other end of the deal, bribed to do another family member's job? Maybe you received no pay at all; maybe you were tricked into the job, as Tom Sawyer tricked his friends into whitewashing a picket fence. Some people are proficient at getting other people to do their work. It chafes at our sense of justice when we see someone unwittingly doing someone else's job. On the other hand we admire and perhaps even stand in awe of a person who willingly assumes a difficult task for someone else.

GROUP DISCUSSION. When have you served as a substitute for someone else? What was the experience like? How adequate did you feel as a substitute? How did others respond to getting you instead of the person they expected?

PERSONAL REFLECTION. When have you wished that someone else would fill in for you and take over your responsibilities? What misgivings did you have about someone taking your place?

There's only one way God could express his holiness without consuming us and express his love without condoning our sins: by providing a divine substitute for the sinner so that the substitute would receive the judgment and the sinner would receive the pardon. The best way to approach the question of substitution for sin is to consider the Old Testament sacrifices, since these were the God-intended preparation for the sacrifice of Christ. Scan Hebrews 9:1-10 for background on the tabernacle (the "pre-temple" place of worship) sacrifices. *Read Hebrews 9:11-28.*

---

1. What contrasts does the writer draw between the earthly sacrifices and the sacrifice of Christ?

---

2. This Scripture passage contains much writing that is visual, helping the reader mentally see what Christ has accomplished. Which word-picture speaks to you most vividly, and why?

---

3. What dual roles did Christ fulfill in his sacrifice (vv. 11, 14)?

---

4. Christ is "the mediator of a new covenant" (v. 15). How is God's mediation different from human ideas of mediation?

---

5. According to this passage, those who enter into Christ's new covenant realize many benefits. What benefits do you find here? How do you see them operating in your life?

6. Christ's death is called a "ransom" (v. 15). How is God's ransom different from our ideas of ransom?

7. Why was blood required for forgiveness and cleansing (vv. 19-22)?

8. Why were animal sacrifices insufficient to deal with human sin?

9. Christ "entered heaven itself" (v. 24). What did he accomplish through his entrance into heaven (vv. 23-26)?

10. How do we know that Christ's sacrifice on the cross was final and does not need to be repeated (vv. 25-26)?

11. What is the certainty of the believer's hope in Christ (vv. 27-28)?

12. What difference does your hope in Christ make in your everyday life, in practical ways?

---

13. Spend a few minutes in quiet reflection on the cross and the self-substitution of God. How have your ideas been challenged or confirmed about Christ and the meaning of the cross in your life?

in the lives of others?

in the world?

Praise the Lord for the extravagant sacrifice of himself. Pray that you will see more clearly both your own unworthiness and the worth he places on you.

Now or Later

The two most outspoken statements of the meaning of Christ's death in Paul's letters are that "Christ redeemed us from the curse of the law by becoming a curse for us" (Galatians 3:13) and that "God made him who had no sin to be sin for us" (2 Corinthians 5:21). Study either or both Scripture passages.

Study a model of the tabernacle to get a more precise understanding of the Holy Place and Most Holy Place. Draw your own conception of the "greater and more perfect tabernacle" not made by human hands (Hebrews 9:11).

7

Justified

The same amount of money for all the workers, whether they started work in the morning or afternoon. A party for the prodigal son. Life instead of a stoning for a woman caught in adultery. In Scripture and still in our world today, people get what they don't deserve. We expect a lecture and receive a raise. We expect the cold shoulder from a friend we ignored and receive an invitation to dinner. To know what we deserve and receive the opposite is a humbling gift—one that helps us know our value in the gift-giver's eyes.

GROUP DISCUSSION. When did you unexpectedly receive something you didn't deserve? How did it come about? What emotions did you experience as a result?

PERSONAL REFLECTION. What things in your past have you had the most trouble believing that God has forgiven? How did you feel toward the Lord when you realized that Christ died for those things as well?

The blessings and consequences of Christ's substitution for us are so richly diverse that they cannot be neatly defined. Several pictures are needed to portray them. One image is that of *justification*, which comes from the law court. Justification is the opposite of condemnation (Romans 5:18; 8:33-34) and both are verdicts of a judge who pronounces the accused either guilty or not guilty. *Justification* bestows on us a righteous standing before God. Some critics dismiss the doctrine as an invention of the apostle Paul, but Paul did not invent the concept. It goes back to Jesus (Luke 18:14) and indeed it goes further back to the Old Testament (Isaiah 53:11). We'll examine it in the book of Titus, Paul's letter to a trusted associate. *Read Titus 3:3-8.*

---

1. What is Paul's mood in this passage, and what gives rise to it?

---

2. When have you shared in Paul's mood, for similar reasons?

---

3. The word *too* (v. 3) may refer to rulers and authorities who do not show exemplary moral character, or it may refer to the human race in general (vv. 1-2). To what extent do you identify with the description in verse 3?

---

4. In two lengthy sentences (vv. 4-7) Paul piles one astonishing fact on top of another. What is his joyful progression of ideas?

---

5. The only negative in verses 4-7 is "not because of righteous things we had done" (v. 5). Why do you think Paul feels obligated to include that phrase?

6. What are the results of our justification (v. 7)?

7. What part does the Holy Spirit play in our salvation (vv. 5-7)?

8. What is the source of our salvation (v. 7)?

9. How does personal justification benefit other people (v. 8)?

10. Christ justifies those who do not deserve it in the least. How do you respond to that idea?

11. Since our justification depends entirely on God's mercy and grace (vv. 5, 7) and is "not because of righteous things we had done" (v. 5), why does Paul ask believers to "be careful to devote themselves to doing what is good" (v. 8)?

12. Spend a few minutes in quiet reflecting on salvation through the cross. How have your ideas about God and the effects of Jesus' work on the cross for your life been challenged or confirmed?

How have your ideas about the effects of Jesus' work on the cross in the lives of others been expanded?

How have your ideas about the effects of the cross in the world been shaped by this text?

Pray your way through Titus 3:4-7, thanking God for each aspect of salvation. Then pray in light of Titus 3:8, asking the Lord to help you devote yourself to doing what is good.

Now or Later

Study Ephesians 1:1-14, another passage in which Paul joyfully praises God for salvation.

Consider ways in which you or your study group can "devote [yourselves] to doing what is good" (Titus 3:8) by ministering to others, especially people outside of your church fellowship(s). Take stock of the gifts and resources you have and the needs that you are aware of. Make specific plans to take action, even in a small way.

In preparation for the next study, read about the glory of God filling the tabernacle in the wilderness (Exodus 40) and the temple in Jerusalem (1 Kings 8).

8

The Revelation of God

Suppose you visit a church whose sign out front proclaims it "The Friendly Church." The same phrase decorates the welcome center in the lobby. It is printed on the gift bag that you receive at the welcome center and on the mug inside the gift bag. "The Friendly Church" is also prominent in the heading of the church bulletin that someone hands you as you enter the sanctuary. It's obvious that this church wants to be thought of as friendly. But how do you know if it truly is a friendly church? Only by one simple test: are the people friendly to you? Their actions will reveal if their church's motto is sincere or only words.

GROUP DISCUSSION. What is one thing you know for sure? How do you know it?

PERSONAL REFLECTION. What does the phrase "the glory of God" mean to you?

The achievement of Christ's cross must be seen in terms of revelation as well as salvation. For through what God did there *for* the world he was also speaking *to* the world. Just as human beings disclose their character in their actions, so God has shown himself to us in the death of his Son. What is striking about John's presentation of Jesus in his Gospel is that, although Jesus' glory was manifested powerfully in his miracles or signs, it was above all to be seen in his weakness, in the self-humiliation of his incarnation. *Read John 1:1-18.*

---

1. Identify all the words and phrases in this passage that have anything to do with knowledge or revelation.

How does this passage help answer someone who says, "We can't know anything for sure about God?"

---

2. What verses and phrases in this passage communicate to you God's love for human beings?

---

3. What do verses 1-4 tell you about the power and authority of the Word (later revealed to be Jesus Christ)?

---

4. How was John the Baptist involved in God's revelation of himself in Christ (vv. 6-8, 15)?

5. Christ is called "the true light" (v. 9). How would you distinguish between a true light and a false light?

6. What is the sharp distinction between those who do and do not recognize and receive Christ (vv. 10-13)?

7. In the Old Testament, God's glory or splendor was revealed in nature and history, that is, in the created universe and in Israel, the redeemed nation. God's glory filled the tabernacle in the wilderness (Exodus 40:34-35) and later the temple in Jerusalem (1 Kings 8:10-11). God displayed his majesty in his world and in his people. According to verse 14, how was the glory of God revealed in a new and startling way?

8. How have you experienced verse 16 in your own life? (Think of recent experiences as well as your own personal history.)

9. How are both *grace* and *truth* revealed in Jesus Christ (vv. 14, 17)?

10. Verse 18 is an unambiguous statement that Christ has made God known. In what senses would you say that you have come to *know* God?

_____

11. What about God is still mysterious to you?

_____

12. Spend a few minutes in quiet reflecting on how God is revealed in the cross of Christ. How have your ideas about God been challenged or confirmed in this study?

What are the implications for your own life?

for how you see others?

Thank God that he has allowed you to come to know him in Jesus, the Word. Pray that you will continue to grow in your knowledge of him.

Now or Later

Discuss or reflect on other ways (besides Christ) that we know about God, such as through nature or our consciences. Consider how Christ is superior to every other avenue of knowledge.

Study 1 John 2:3-5; 4:7-21 concerning the practical results of knowing God in Christ. Evaluate the evidence that you truly know God. Pray about internal and external changes that you want the Holy Spirit to make in your life.

9

The Conquest
of Evil

Colossians 2:6-15

It is impossible to read the New Testament without being impressed by the atmosphere of joyful confidence that pervades it, which stands out in relief against the rather deflated religion that often passes for Christianity today. As the twenty-first-century world appears to get worse and worse, some Christians regard the situation as hopeless. They pull back into isolation, waiting only for Christ to return. By contrast, there was no defeatism about the early Christians; they spoke rather of victory: the Crucified was actually a conqueror.

GROUP DISCUSSION. When you see or hear the word *evil,* how do you react? What images come to mind?

PERSONAL REFLECTION. When you think about the power of evil in the world, do you feel mostly hopeful or mostly discouraged? Why?

What the New Testament affirms, in its own uninhibited way, is that at the cross Jesus disarmed and triumphed over the devil and all the "principalities and powers" at his command. This victory of Christ is set forth especially powerfully in Colossians 2:13-15, as you'll see. *Read Colossians 2:6-15.*

1. What warnings as well as reasons for hope are expressed in this passage?

_____

2. How much do you personally identify with the hope of this passage?

_____

3. How much do you personally feel vulnerable to the risks in this passage?

_____

4. What is the logical connection between the assurance of verses 6-7 and the warning of verse 8?

_____

5. Paul says confidently that believers have entered into the fullness of God in Christ, "who is the head over every power and authority" (vv. 9-10). What are the implications for how we should view and deal with evil?

_____

6. Circumcision was the God-given covenant sign of being a Jew, one of God's chosen people (Genesis 17:9-14). In verses 11-12 Paul refers to a new, nonphysical circumcision done by Christ, and to baptism as a symbol of burial and resurrection. How do all these word-pictures confirm our participation in the fullness of Christ (vv. 9-10)?

_____

7. According to verses 13-14, how did Christ deal with our sin?

8. How did Christ deal with the powers of evil (v. 15)?

_____

9. When have you seen evil decisively defeated by the power of Christ?

_____

10. Where do you see evil still apparently reigning?

_____

11. How might God be leading you to be involved in his conquest of evil?

_____

12. Spend a few minutes in quiet reflecting on Christ's victory over evil. How does the cross give you hope in the face of evil?

Pray against the evil you see in your community, the larger society, the world—and in your own life. Thank God for his victory both present and future.

Now or Later

Study Colossians 1:15-20 and Ephesians 1:15-23 concerning Christ's victory and supremacy over all other powers.

Look for articles and other information about Christian organizations involved in bringing justice to the world. Discuss how you or your group can support one or more of these ministries.

Discuss ways you can combat evil in your own community, not in a judgmental way but in the joyful and Christlike spirit of Colossians.

10

The Community
of Celebration

Perhaps you have so far found this presentation of Christ's cross too individualistic. If so, this study should restore the balance. The purpose of Christ's self-giving on the cross was not just to save isolated individuals but to create a new community—whose members would belong to him, love one another and eagerly serve the world. The community of Christ will be nothing less than a renewed and reunited humanity, which Christ, as the second Adam, will head (1 Corinthians 15:45).

GROUP DISCUSSION. Consider your own church fellowship(s). Do you chiefly think of yourselves as part of the community of Christ? What other identities might compete with your principal identity as the community of Christ?

PERSONAL REFLECTION. How vital has Christian fellowship been to your own spiritual growth? How important do you see yourself in the spiritual growth of others?

From the Day of Pentecost onward (Acts 2), it has been clear that conversion to Christ means also conversion to the community of Christ.

These two transfers—of personal allegiance and social member-ship—cannot be separated. *Read 1 Peter 2:4-10,* written by the apostle who preached powerfully on that Day of Pentecost.

---

1. What terms does Peter use in this passage to identify the people who belong to Christ?

---

2. How fully and accurately does this passage reflect your own expe-rience in Christ?

---

3. Which picture of the Christian community in this passage speaks most deeply to you, and why?

---

4. What is the relationship of the "living stones" to the "living Stone" (vv. 4-5)?

---

5. The uniqueness of Christ's sacrifice on the cross does not mean that we have no sacrifices to offer, but only that their nature and purpose are different. They are not material but spiritual, and their object is not *propitiatory* (turning away God's wrath) but *eucharistic* (thanksgiving), the expression of a responsive gratitude. What would be some examples of "spiritual sacrifices" (v. 5)?

---

6. Verses 6-8 include three Old Testament quotes that are applied to Christ. How and why does the *stone* affect different people in differ-ent ways?

7. According to verses 9-10, in what ways are believers different from the rest of humanity?

---

8. We have received mercy so that we may "declare the praises of him who called [us] out of darkness into his wonderful light" (v. 9). Our new intimate relationship to God, which has replaced the old and painful estrangement, is marked by boldness, love and joy. These are not to be thought of as purely private and interior experiences; they are to distinguish our public worship. Consider your public worship with other believers. What aspects of your worship express

boldness?

love?

joy?

---

9. How large a part does thanksgiving play in the worship in your church fellowship? Consider all elements that might incorporate thankfulness to God, including prayer, singing, offerings, Scripture reading, Communion and preaching.

---

10. Peter specifically identifies Christians as the people of God (v. 10). What ungodly influences on the church threaten to dilute our identity as the people of God?

---

11. In verse 10 Peter also identifies Christians as people who have received mercy. What implications do you see for how believers should regard one another?

12. What reasons do you hear from people who feel they don't need to be part of a church to have a relationship with Christ?

13. Spend a few minutes in quiet reflecting on your own part in the community of Christ. How have your ideas about church been challenged or confirmed in this study?

What are the implications for your own life?

for how you see others in your fellowship?

Thank God for your fellowship of believers. Ask forgiveness for any petty criticisms of other Christians that you tend to make. Pray for the Holy Spirit to protect your fellowship from sin, and to make you bold and joyful in declaring the gospel.

Now or Later

Choose a stone to represent the "living Stone" of 1 Peter 2:4. Use a marker to write on it the scriptural names of Christ or some of Christ's attributes. Arrange smaller stones around this stone to represent yourselves as "living stones" in relation to Christ. Write the names of your group members on the smaller stones. Have each group member take a small stone and pray for that person this week. If you are doing this study independently, write the names of some other people in your church who have particular needs, and pray for them this week.

Study Paul's picture of the church as the body of Christ in 1 Corinthians 12.

Study one or more of the spiritual sacrifices mentioned in Scripture (see the leader's note for question 5).

11

Self-Understanding and Self-Giving

A popular singer was asked what would be an ideal day for her. She replied that on a perfect day she would get up in the morning and eat whatever she wanted. This young woman left the sad impression that her image-makers tell her what to eat and what not to eat. She has reached the top of her career, and if she wants to stay there she must conform to an external standard. Meanwhile, who is she on the inside? Her fans do not know, and perhaps at this point she does not even know.

GROUP DISCUSSION. What do you think is the healthiest attitude for people to have toward themselves? How can people arrive at that attitude?

PERSONAL REFLECTION. Do you think your evaluation of yourself tends to be too low or too high, and why? How has your evaluation of yourself varied at different times in your life?

The cross revolutionizes our attitude toward ourselves as well as toward God. The community of the cross, in addition to being a community of celebration, is also one of self-understanding. We are new people because we have died and risen with Christ. Our old life of sin, guilt and shame has ended, and a new life of holiness, forgiveness and freedom has begun. But because our new self, though redeemed, is still fallen, a double attitude will be necessary, namely, self-denial and self-affirmation, both illumined by the cross.

Right after Peter had acknowledged Jesus as the Christ and Jesus had predicted his own suffering and death, Jesus addressed the first of these two attitudes: self-denial. *Read Luke 9:23-27.*

1. In a word or phrase, what is Jesus asking of his disciples?

2. What contemporary ideas of *self* does Jesus contradict in this passage?

3. How do you react to this Scripture?

4. When you think of denying yourself (9:23) what images come to mind?

5. How do you interpret the idea of taking up your cross daily (9:23)?

6. How would you summarize the paradox of Luke 9:24-25?

7. What examples of Luke 9:24-25 (either positive or negative) have you observed?

8. How might trying to "save" our life cause us to become "ashamed" of Jesus (9:26-27)?

Alongside Jesus' explicit call to self-denial is his implicit call to self-affirmation (which is not at all the same thing as self-love). *Read Luke 12:22-34.*

9. Identify all the promises of God in this Scripture passage.

How have you found the promises here to be true?

10. Based on this passage, what is the value that God places on humans?

11. Spend a few minutes in quiet reflecting on your own understanding of yourself in light of the cross. How have your ideas about yourself been challenged or confirmed?

Thank the Lord for courageously carrying the literal cross and fulfilling his mission to die there. Pray that you will daily take up your own cross, die to self and live to him. Thank him that he cares for you and will supply all your needs, physical and spiritual.

Now or Later

Study Paul's declaration that "I have been crucified with Christ" in Galatians 2:17-21.

Draw a cross and write on it your most persistent temptations to live for yourself rather than for Christ. Have a time of prayer and commitment that you will take up your cross daily and follow Christ.

As an act of thankfulness, plan ways you or your group can share God's material and spiritual blessings with others.

12

Loving Our Enemies

Romans 12:9; 12:14—13:5

When hurt or cheated by someone else, who hasn't felt the desire to get even? Some people try to settle the score right away. Others bide their time and wait for the right opportunity. The words *get even* seem to express a desire for fair play. If one side has been unfairly beaten down, and then the score is evened up, it would appear that justice has been done. Yet, whether or not we look at getting even as a form of justice, one thing is certain: the offender and the offended will remain unreconciled. The person who tries to get even is not interested in making an enemy into a friend.

GROUP DISCUSSION. Consider this question: does the cross commit us to a nonviolent acceptance of all violence?

PERSONAL REFLECTION. When you think of your "enemies," who or what do you think of? When and how have you been able to love an enemy? What enemy do you still find it difficult to love?

To "live under the cross" means that every aspect of the Christian community's life is shaped by it. The cross directs our conduct in relation to others, including our enemies. We are to exhibit in our relationships that combination of love and justice which characterized the wisdom of God in the cross. But how, in practice, we are to combine love and justice, mercy and severity is often hard to decide and harder still to do. Romans 12—13, part of Paul's plea to his Christian readers to live "in view of God's mercy" (Romans 12:1), gives us some helpful instructions. *Read Romans 12:9, 14-21.*

---

1. Based on this passage, what general statements can you make about how a Christian should respond to evil?

---

2. What is your reaction to Paul's advice here?

How do you think the Roman Christians receiving this letter reacted to Paul's words?

---

3. Hate (v. 9) sounds like an un-Christian attitude. What do you think it means to "hate what is evil"?

---

4. What would it be like to live in a society characterized by Romans 12:14-16?

---

5. What do the four "do nots" in Romans 12:14, 17-21 have in common?

---

6. The four "do nots" all have a positive counterpart. What do the four positives have in common?

If we were to stop our consideration of evil at this point, we would be guilty of grave biblical selectivity and imbalance. For Paul goes on to write of the punishment of evil by the state. *Read Romans 13:1-5.*

7. What are Paul's reasons for submitting to civil authorities?

8. What is the state's role in restraining evil?

9. How does this passage from Romans 13 add to your understanding of how a Christian should respond to evil?

10. When and how are you most tempted to take matters into your own hands and retaliate?

11. Spend a few minutes in quiet reflecting on loving your enemies. In light of the cross what is God calling you to do or understand about your enemies?

Pray silently for anyone you would consider an "enemy." Pray together for Christian love for your enemies. Pray also for those who work in law enforcement, and in other ways, to restrain evil in society.

Now or Later

Study 1 Peter 2:13-25 concerning a Christlike attitude toward authority, whether good or bad.

Since the next study is your final one, consider a special time of worship centered around the cross.

13

Suffering and Glory

The fact of suffering undoubtedly constitutes the single greatest challenge to the Christian faith, and it's been present in every generation. Its distribution and degree appear to be entirely random and therefore unfair. Many ask if it can possibly be reconciled with God's justice and love. It is the old conundrum that God is either not good or not almighty. Either he wants to stop suffering but cannot, or he could but will not. Whichever it is, how can we worship him as God?

It needs to be said at once that the Bible supplies no thorough solution to the problem of evil, whether natural evil or moral, that is, whether in the form of suffering or of sin. Though there are references to sin and suffering on virtually every page, the Bible's concern is not to explain their origin but to help us overcome them. The object of this study is to explore what relation there might be between the cross of Christ and our sufferings.

GROUP DISCUSSION. What is the worst thing about suffering? What are some possible redeeming qualities of suffering?

PERSONAL REFLECTION. What have you learned through suffering?

What is the relationship between Christ's sufferings and ours? How does the cross speak to us in our pain? *Read Hebrews 4:14-16; 5:7-9.*

1. From this Scripture, what new insights into the suffering of Jesus do you gain?

2. What does it mean to you to know that our high priest Jesus is able to sympathize with us (4:14-15)?

3. What does it mean to you to know that we can now approach God's throne with confidence (4:16)?

4. This Scripture seems to refer specifically to Jesus' prayers in Gethsemane just before he was arrested, although it may refer to his entire life on earth. What did Jesus' suffering accomplish in his own life?

5. What did Jesus' suffering accomplish for humanity?

6. In your own experience, how has suffering given you sympathy for others?

7. How has suffering helped your spiritual maturity?

8. How has the patient suffering of other Christians deepened your respect for them?

---

9. What does the suffering of Jesus tell you about God?

---

10. When have you especially felt that Christ was with you in your suffering?

---

11. Spend a few minutes in quiet reflecting on the cross of Christ and what it says to you about suffering, both your own and that of others.

Pray for all you know who are suffering. Thank God for not standing aloof from pain but being a God who suffered and continues to suffer. Thank him for lessons learned through suffering.

Now or Later

Discuss this statement: "I could never myself believe in God if it were not for the cross. In the real world of pain, how could one worship a God who was immune to it?" Do you agree or disagree, and why?

No matter what subject or Scripture you study next, resolve to keep asking the question "How does this relate to the cross?"

Leader's Notes

Leading a Bible discussion can be an enjoyable and rewarding experience. But it can also be scary especially if you've never done it before. If this is your feeling, you're in good company. When God asked Moses to lead the Israelites out of Egypt, he replied, "O Lord, please send someone else to do it!" (Ex 4:13). It was the same with Solomon, Jeremiah and Timothy, but God helped these people in spite of their weaknesses, and he will help you as well.

You don't need to be an expert on the Bible or a trained teacher to lead a Bible discussion. The idea behind these inductive studies is that the leader guides group members to discover for themselves what the Bible has to say. This method of learning will allow group members to remember much more of what is said than a lecture would.

These studies are designed to be led easily. As a matter of fact, the flow of questions through the passage from observation to interpretation to application is so natural that you may feel that the studies lead themselves. This study guide is also flexible. You can use it with a variety of groups student, professional, neighborhood or church groups. Each study takes forty-five to sixty minutes in a group setting.

There are some important facts to know about group dynamics and encouraging discussion. The suggestions listed below should enable you to effectively and enjoyably fulfill your role as leader.

Preparing for the Study

1. Ask God to help you understand and apply the passage in your own life. Unless this happens, you will not be prepared to lead others. Pray too for the various members of the group. Ask God to open your hearts to the message of his Word and motivate you to action.

2. Read the introduction to the entire guide to get an overview of the entire book and the issues which will be explored.

3. As you begin each study, read and reread the assigned Bible passage to familiarize yourself with it.

4. This study guide is based on the New International Version of the Bible. It will help you and the group if you use this translation as the basis for your study and discussion.

5. Carefully work through each question in the study. Spend time in meditation and reflection as you consider how to respond.

6. Write your thoughts and responses in the space provided in the study guide. This will help you to express your understanding of the passage clearly.

7. It might help to have a Bible dictionary handy. Use it to look up any unfamiliar words, names or places. (For additional help on how to study a passage, see chapter five of *How to Lead a LifeGuide Bible Study*, InterVarsity Press.)

8. Consider how you can apply the Scripture to your life. Remember that the group will follow your lead in responding to the studies. They will not go any deeper than you do.

9. Once you have finished your own study of the passage, familiarize yourself with the leader's notes for the study you are leading. These are designed to help you in several ways. First, they tell you the purpose the study guide author had in mind when writing the study. Take time to think through how the study questions work together to accomplish that purpose. Second, the notes provide you with additional background information or suggestions on group dynamics for various questions. This information can be useful when people have difficulty understanding or answering a question. Third, the leader's notes can alert you to potential problems you may encounter during the study.

10. If you wish to remind yourself of anything mentioned in the leader's notes, make a note to yourself below that question in the study.

Leading the Study

1. Begin the study on time. Open with prayer, asking God to help the group to understand and apply the passage.

2. Be sure that everyone in your group has a study guide. Encourage the group to prepare beforehand for each discussion by reading the introduction to the guide and by working through the questions in the study.

3. At the beginning of your first time together, explain that these studies are meant to be discussions, not lectures. Encourage the members of the group to participate. However, do not put pressure on those who may be hesitant to speak during the first few sessions. You may want to suggest the following guidelines to your group.

☐ Stick to the topic being discussed.

☐ Your responses should be based on the verses which are the focus of the discussion and not on outside authorities such as commentaries or speakers.

☐ These studies focus on a particular passage of Scripture. Only rarely should you refer to other portions of the Bible. This allows for everyone to participate in in-depth study on equal ground.

☐ Anything said in the group is considered confidential and will not be discussed outside the group unless specific permission is given to do so.

☐ We will listen attentively to each other and provide time for each person present to talk.

☐ We will pray for each other.

4. Have a group member read the introduction at the beginning of the discussion.

5. Every session begins with a group discussion question. The question or activity is meant to be used before the passage is read. The question introduces the theme of the study and encourages group members to begin to open up. Encourage as many members as possible to participate, and be ready to get the discussion going with your own response.

This section is designed to reveal where our thoughts or feelings need to be transformed by Scripture. That is why it is especially important not to read the passage before the discussion question is asked. The passage will tend to color the honest reactions people would otherwise give because they are, of course, supposed to think the way the Bible does.

You may want to supplement the group discussion question with an icebreaker to help people to get comfortable. See the community section of *Small Group Idea Book* for more ideas.

You also might want to use the personal reflection question with your group. Either allow a time of silence for people to respond individually or discuss it together.

6. Have a group member (or members if the passage is long) read aloud the passage to be studied. Then give people several minutes to read the passage again silently so that they can take it all in.

7. Question 1 will generally be an overview question designed to briefly survey the passage. Encourage the group to look at the whole passage, but try to avoid getting sidetracked by questions or issues that will be addressed later in the study.

8. As you ask the questions, keep in mind that they are designed to be used just as they are written. You may simply read them aloud. Or you may prefer to express them in your own words.

There may be times when it is appropriate to deviate from the study guide. For example, a question may have already been answered. If so, move on to the next question. Or someone may raise an important question not covered in the guide. Take time to discuss it, but try to keep the group from going off on tangents.

9. Avoid answering your own questions. If necessary, repeat or rephrase

them until they are clearly understood. Or point out something you read in the leader's notes to clarify the context or meaning. An eager group quickly becomes passive and silent if they think the leader will do most of the talking.

10. Don't be afraid of silence. People may need time to think about the question before formulating their answers.

11. Don't be content with just one answer. Ask, "What do the rest of you think?" or "Anything else?" until several people have given answers to the question.

12. Acknowledge all contributions. Try to be affirming whenever possible. Never reject an answer. If it is clearly off-base, ask, "Which verse led you to that conclusion?" or again, "What do the rest of you think?"

13. Don't expect every answer to be addressed to you, even though this will probably happen at first. As group members become more at ease, they will begin to truly interact with each other. This is one sign of healthy discussion.

14. Don't be afraid of controversy. It can be very stimulating. If you don't resolve an issue completely, don't be frustrated. Move on and keep it in mind for later. A subsequent study may solve the problem.

15. Periodically summarize what the group has said about the passage. This helps to draw together the various ideas mentioned and gives continuity to the study. But don't preach.

16. At the end of the Bible discussion you may want to allow group members a time of quiet to work on an idea under "Now or Later." Then discuss what you experienced. Or you may want to encourage group members to work on these ideas between meetings. Give an opportunity during the session for people to talk about what they are learning.

17. Conclude your time together with conversational prayer, adapting the prayer suggestion at the end of the study to your group. Ask for God's help in following through on the commitments you've made.

18. End on time.

Many more suggestions and helps are found in *How to Lead a LifeGuide Bible Study.*

Components of Small Groups

A healthy small group should do more than study the Bible. There are four components to consider as you structure your time together.

Nurture. Small groups help us to grow in our knowledge and love of God. Bible study is the key to making this happen and is the foundation of your small group.

Community. Small groups are a great place to develop deep friendships with other Christians. Allow time for informal interaction before and after each study. Plan activities and games that will help you get to know each other. Spend time having fun together going on a picnic or cooking dinner together.

Worship and prayer. Your study will be enhanced by spending time praising God together in prayer or song. Pray for each other's needs and keep track of how God is answering prayer in your group. Ask God to help you to apply what you are learning in your study.

Outreach. Reaching out to others can be a practical way of applying what you are learning, and it will keep your group from becoming self-focused. Host a series of evangelistic discussions for your friends or neighbors. Clean up the yard of an elderly friend. Serve at a soup kitchen together, or spend a day working on a Habitat house.

Many more suggestions and helps in each of these areas are found in *Small Group Idea Book*. Information on building a small group can be found in *Small Group Leaders' Handbook* and *The Big Book on Small Groups* (both from InterVarsity Press). Reading through one of these books would be worth your time.

Study 1. The Centrality of the Cross. Isaiah 53.
Purpose: To affirm the cross of Christ as the center of the Christian faith.

Group discussion. Here's an alternate or additional question if you have time: Human beings are made in such a way that we can remember the past, but we cannot see into the future. Imagine that it's the other way around: we know what will happen in the future, but we can remember nothing. How would our lives be different? What advantages would there be? What disadvantages would there be?

Background note. Isaiah 53 is often read in churches during Advent because it anticipates the coming of the Messiah. Although written several centuries before Christ, it offers an intensely moving picture of Christ's sufferings and triumph.

Question 1. Accept all responses from participants. As a follow-up question, ask "What common thread do we find in all these ideas?" or "How can we tie all these ideas together in a few words?"

Question 3. It's not just the images Isaiah presents that might be hard to believe but the fact that God himself would come to earth to save human beings. One commentator says, "We could suitably paraphrase Isaiah: 'Who could have believed that this was the Arm of the Lord?', i.e. the Lord himself come to act in salvation" (J. Alec Motyer, *Isaiah,* Tyndale Old Testament Commentaries [Leicester, U.K.: Inter-Varsity Press, 1999], p. 333).

In addition, the Israelites, as God's people, had the task of witnessing to other nations that the Lord is God, but they were frequently "blind and deaf" to this calling. Isaiah reveals his confidence that the Israelites will not just witness to the fact that the Lord is God; they'll also "witness to his saving power revealed in the suffering, death and exaltation of the Servant" (Barry G. Webb, *The Message of Isaiah,* The Bible Speaks Today [Downers Grove, Ill.: InterVarsity Press, 1996], pp. 210-11).

Question 5. Although the apostles attributed the death of Jesus to human wickedness, they declared that it was also due to a divine purpose. Moreover, what God had foreknown, he had foretold. So the apostles repeatedly emphasized that the death and resurrection of Jesus happened "according to the Scriptures." When we turn from the apostles' early sermons recorded in the Acts to their letters, the prominent place they give to the cross is even more marked. Paul, Peter and John are unanimous in witnessing to its centrality, as are also the letter to the Hebrews and Revelation.

Question 6. Responses could include those who have infirmities and sorrow (v. 4), those who are guilty of transgressions and iniquities (v. 5), and those who are going astray like sheep (v. 6).

Question 7. For the Lord's silence before his accusers (Is 53:7) see Matthew 27:12-14; Mark 14:57-61; Luke 23:8-9. At times during his trial Jesus did speak out, but at other times he maintained a deliberate and dignified silence.

Question 9. The Servant's life becomes "a guilt offering" (v. 10); he "will justify many, / and he will bear their iniquities" (v. 11); "he bore the sin of many, / and made intercession for the transgressors" (v. 12). As a possible follow-up question, ask, "How do you respond to the idea in verse 10 that 'it was the Lord's will to crush him and cause him to suffer'?"

Question 10. It seems definite that Jesus applied Isaiah 53 to himself and understood his death as a sin-bearing death. As God's "righteous servant" he would be able to "justify many" because he was going to "bear the sin of many."

Paul, Peter, Matthew, Luke and John together allude to at least eight of the twelve verses in Isaiah 53. What was the origin of their confident, detailed application of Isaiah 53 to Jesus? They must have derived it from his own lips. The only straight quotation of Isaiah 53 that is recorded from Jesus is from verse 12, when Jesus said "I tell you that this must be fulfilled in me" (Lk 22:37). Nevertheless, he declared that he "must suffer many things" and did "not come to be served, but to serve, and to give his life as a ransom for many" (Mk 8:31; 10:45). Although these are not direct quotations from Isaiah 53, their combined themes of suffering, service and death for the salvation of others point in that direction.

Question 11. Possible answers could be loving your fellow human beings, doing good works, demonstrating upright moral character, accepting Christ as Savior, having faith, sending out missionaries and so on.

Question 13. This question is an opportunity for group members to privately reflect on the study. A similar question will appear at the end of each study. People may want to write down some of their thoughts in their study guide or in a journal. Then you can discuss them together. Assure group members that they will not be asked to read their journals aloud, although they may choose to do so.

Study 2. Why Did Christ Die? Matthew 27:11-26.
Purpose: To identify the forces that sent Jesus to the cross.
Question 1. It was customary for the governor to release one prisoner at Passover. Pilate offered to release Jesus (vv. 15-17) but gave in to the crowd's demand for Barabbas (vv. 20-23). Pilate ignored his wife's warning message in which she called Jesus "that innocent man" (v. 19). He put up mild resistance to the crowd's demand for Jesus' crucifixion (vv. 22-23) but then literally washed his hands of the matter (v. 24). Luke also tells us that Pilate tried to transfer Jesus' case to Herod (Lk 23:5-12) and offered to have Jesus illegally flogged, although he was innocent (Lk 23:16, 22).
Question 2. Pilate is known to have been appointed procurator (Roman governor) of the border province of Judea by the Emperor Tiberius and to have served for ten years from about A.D. 26 to 36. He acquired a reputation as an able administrator with a typically Roman sense of fair play. But he was hated by the Jews because he was contemptuous of them. According to Philo, King Agrippa I described him in a letter to the Emperor Caligula as "a man of very inflexible disposition, and very merciless as well as very obstinate." Pilate's overriding aim was to maintain law and order, to keep the Jews firmly under control and, if necessary, to ruthlessly suppress any riot or threat of one. The portrait of Pontius Pilate in the Gospels tallies well with the external evidence.
Question 4. It is easy to condemn Pilate and overlook our own equally devious behavior. Anxious to avoid the pain of wholehearted commitment to Christ, we too search for convenient subterfuges. We either leave the decision to somebody else, opt for half-hearted compromise, seek to honor Jesus for the wrong reason (as teacher instead of as Lord) or even make a public affirmation of loyalty while at the same time denying him in our hearts.
Question 5. Envy is the reverse of vanity. We are not envious of others unless we are first proud of ourselves. The Jewish leaders were proud of their nation's long history of a special relationship with God, of their own leadership role in this nation and, above all, of their authority. Their contest with Jesus was essentially an authority struggle.

Jesus had upset the Jewish establishment from the outset of his public ministry. He challenged their authority and possessed an authority that they lacked. He undermined their prestige, their hold over the people, and their self-confidence and self-respect, while leaving his own intact. He had no credentials. He courted controversy by fraternizing with disreputable people, feasting instead of fasting and profaning the sabbath by healing people on it. He had even made outrageous claims to be lord of the sabbath, to know God uniquely as his Father, even to be equal with God. The Jewish leaders had good political, theological and ethical reasons for demanding that he be arrested, put on trial and silenced.

Yet there were flaws in the Jewish leaders' case. Was it entirely that they were concerned for political stability, doctrinal truth and moral purity? Pilate did not think so. There is no reason to question Pilate's assessment. He was a shrewd judge of human character. Besides, the Gospel writers appear, by recording his judgment, to endorse it.

Question 6. The same envy influences our contemporary attitudes toward Jesus. We resent his intrusions into our privacy, his demand for our homage, his expectation of our obedience. Western culture intensifies our drive for independence. We do not want to be dependent on anyone, and we resist any authority whom we think threatens our individual rights. To these objections Jesus instantly replies that we are his business and that he will never leave us alone. So we too perceive him as a threatening rival who disturbs our peace, upsets our status quo, undermines our authority and diminishes our self-respect. We too want to get rid of him.

Question 7. Pilate tried to proclaim his own innocence. And then, before his hands were dry, he handed Jesus over to be crucified. You might ask as a follow-up question how he could bring himself to incur this great guilt immediately after proclaiming his innocence.

Question 8. Some blame the Jewish people for the crucifixion of Jesus. The way to avoid anti-Semitic prejudice is not to pretend that the Jews were innocent, but, having admitted their guilt, to add that others shared in it. This is how the apostles saw it. Herod and Pilate, Gentiles and Jews, they said, had together "conspired" against Jesus (Acts 4:27). More important still, we are also guilty because of our sin.

Question 9. On the human level, Judas gave Jesus up to the priests, who gave him up to Pilate, who gave him up to the soldiers, who crucified him. On the divine level, the Father gave him up, and he gave himself up, to die for us.

We too, though, were participants on the human level: guilty participants plotting, scheming, betraying, bargaining and handing him over to be crucified. We may try to wash our hands of responsibility like Pilate. But our attempts will be as futile as his. For there is blood on our hands.

As we face the cross, then, we can say to ourselves both "I did it, my sins sent him there" and "he did it, his love took him there."

Study 3. Looking Below the Surface. Mark 14:12-26.
Purpose: To discern the purposes of God in the crucifixion of Christ.

Background note. Reading Exodus 11—12 before you lead this study might be helpful for your group discussion time.

Question 1. Jesus had no family home in Jerusalem and apparently none of his disciples did either, at least not a home where they could celebrate the Passover in seclusion. Jesus arranged with someone in Jerusalem to borrow an upper room in a house. He also arranged for covert signals to lead his disciples to the place. In these careful arrangements and in the manner he presided over the Passover meal, even as he demonstrated the symbols of his own approaching death, he showed an extraordinary sense of purposeful calm.

Question 4. Jesus reinterpreted the bread and wine of the Passover as his own body and blood. The "blood" would have been especially unsettling to the disciples because the first Passover involved putting the blood of a lamb on the doorframes of Hebrew homes. Christ was comparing himself with the slain Passover lamb.

Questions 5-6. The bread did not stand for Jesus' living body as he reclined with them at table, but his body as it was shortly to be given for them in death. He broke the bread as his own body would soon be broken. Luke adds Jesus' instructions "Do this in remembrance of me" (Lk 22:19).

The wine did not stand for his blood as it flowed in his veins while he spoke to them, but his blood that was shortly to be poured out in death for them. According to Paul and Matthew, Jesus' words about the cup referred not only to his blood but to the new covenant associated with his blood; Matthew adds further that his blood was to be shed "for the forgiveness of sins" (see Mt 26:27-29; 1 Cor 11:23-26).

Many centuries prior, God had entered into a covenant with Abraham (Gen 15). God renewed the covenant at Mt. Sinai after rescuing Israel from Egypt (Ex 19:1-6). Moses sprinkled the people with bull's blood, which he called "the blood of the covenant" (Ex 24:8). Hundreds of years passed in which the people forsook God, broke his covenant and provoked his judgment, until the word of the Lord came to the prophet Jeremiah, who announced that the Lord would make a new covenant on the people's hearts (Jer 31:31-34).

More than six centuries later, Jesus dared to say, in effect: "The new covenant is about to be established; the forgiveness of sins promised as one of its distinctive blessings is about to become available; and the sacrifice to seal this covenant and procure this forgiveness will be the shedding of my blood in death." Is it possible to exaggerate the staggering nature of this claim? He was going to die in order to bring his people into a new covenant relationship with God.

Unfortunately, we can get so familiar with Jesus' words regarding the bread and wine that they tend to lose their impact. Yet they throw floods of light on Jesus' own view of his death.

Question 7. The answer is so obvious that it may be missed: they eat the bread and drink the wine. Jesus was giving an advance dramatization of his death. The drama did not consist of one actor on the stage with a dozen in the audience. No, it involved the disciples as well as him, so that they all took part in it. True, he took, blessed and broke the bread, but then he explained its significance as he gave it to them to eat. Again he took and blessed the cup, but then he explained its meaning as he gave it to them to drink. Just as it was not enough for the bread to be broken and the wine to be poured out (the disciples had to eat and drink), it is not enough for him to die; we have to appropriate the benefits of his death personally.

The eating and drinking were, and still are, a vivid parable of receiving Christ as our crucified Savior and of feeding on him in our hearts by faith. For Christ to give his body and blood in death was one thing; for us to make the blessings of his death our own is another. The Lord's Supper remains the perpetual outward sign of both the divine gift and its human reception. It is intended to be a participation in the body and blood of Christ (1 Cor 10:16).

Question 8. The Mount of Olives was where Jesus and his disciples were customarily spending the night during their time in Jerusalem (Lk 21:37). The Garden of Gethsemane was there (Mk 14:32). It was typically a place of safety and seclusion.

Question 9. The cross enforces three truths—about ourselves, about God and about Jesus Christ.

First, our sin must be extremely horrible. Nothing reveals the gravity of sin like the cross. If there is no way by which the righteous God could righteously forgive our unrighteousness, except by bearing it himself in Christ, it must be serious indeed.

Second, God's love must be wonderful beyond comprehension. He pursued us even to the desolate anguish of the cross, where he bore our sin, guilt, judgment and death. It takes a hard and stony heart to remain unmoved by love like that. Its proper name is grace, which is love to the undeserving.

Third, Christ's salvation must be a free gift. He "purchased" it for us as the high price of his own lifeblood (Rev 5:9). What is there left for us to pay? Nothing!

Study 4. The Problem of Forgiveness. Romans 2:1-11.

Purpose: To acknowledge the inevitable collision between God's holiness and humans' rebellion.

General note. Paul's word "therefore" (v. 1) refers to his previous argument that those without God's law (Gentiles) are still morally responsible and guilty because "what may be known about God is plain to them, because God has made it plain to them" (Rom 1:19).

Question 2. Paul uncovers in these verses a strange human foible, namely, our tendency to be critical of everybody except ourselves. We are often as harsh in our judgment of others as we are lenient toward ourselves. Paul argues that we expose ourselves to the judgment of God and we leave ourselves without either excuse or escape.

Question 3. The essential background to the cross is not only the sin, responsibility and guilt of human beings but the just reaction of God to these things, in other words, his holiness and wrath. What is common to the biblical concepts of the holiness and the wrath of God is the truth that neither of them can coexist with sin.

That God is holy is foundational to biblical religion. So is the corollary that sin is incompatible with his holiness. His eyes are "too pure to look on evil" and he "cannot tolerate wrong" (Hab 1:13). Therefore our sins effectively separate us from him, so that his face is hidden from us and he refuses to listen to our prayers (Is 59:1-2).

Closely related to God's holiness is his wrath, his holy reaction to evil. We certainly cannot dismiss it by saying that the God of wrath belongs to the Old Testament while the God of the New Testament is love. For God's love is clearly seen in the Old Testament, as is his wrath in the New.

Question 4. Romans 2:1-4 comes in the context of Paul's extended argument throughout chapters 1—3 that all of humanity is under the judgment of God. Paul writes of Gentiles without the law that "what may be known about God is plain to them, because God has made it plain to them . . . so that people are without excuse" (Rom 1:19-20 TNIV). He writes to the self-righteous, whether Jew or Gentile, that "you are condemning yourself, because you who pass judgment do the same things" (Rom 2:1). He writes to Jews who know the law, "You who brag about the law, do you dishonor God by breaking the law?" (Rom 2:23). Finally he writes of humanity as a whole: "There is no difference, for all have sinned and fall short of the glory of God" (Rom 3:22-23).

Questions 9-10. Does Paul declare that salvation is by faith alone and then destroy his own gospel by saying that it is by good works after all? No, Paul is not contradicting himself. Although justification is indeed by faith, judgment will be according to works. The Day of Judgment will be a public occasion. Its purpose will be less to determine God's judgment than to announce it and to vindicate it. The divine judgment, which is a process of sifting and separating, is going on secretly all the time as people arrange themselves for or against Christ, but on the last day its results will be made public (Mt 25:31-46).

Such a public occasion, on which a public verdict will be given and a public sentence passed, will require public and verifiable evidence to support them. The only public evidence available will be our works, what we have done and have been seen to do (Jas 2:14-16). The presence or absence of saving faith in our hearts will be disclosed by the presence or absence of good works of love in our lives (see Rev 20:11-15).

Question 12. The problem of forgiveness is constituted by the inevitable collision between divine perfection and human sin, between God as he is and us as we are. The obstacle to forgiveness is neither our sin alone nor our guilt alone, but also the divine reaction in love and wrath toward guilty sinners. Although "God is love" (1 Jn 4:8, 16), we have to remember that his love is holy love, love which yearns over sinners and desires for them to be free from sin while at the same time refusing to condone their sin.

At the cross, in holy love, God through Christ paid the full penalty of our disobedience himself. He bore the judgment we deserve in order to bring us the forgiveness we do not deserve. On the cross divine mercy and justice were equally expressed and eternally reconciled.

Study 5. Satisfaction for Sin. Romans 3:19-26.

Purpose: To see that both the justice of God and the love of God were satisfied by God himself on the cross.

Question 4. The purpose of the law was to lift the lid off human respectability and disclose what we are really like underneath—sinful, rebellious, guilty, under the judgment of God and helpless to save ourselves. The law must still be allowed to do its God-given duty today. We will not appreciate the gospel until the law has first revealed us to ourselves. Not until the law has bruised and smitten us will we admit our need of the gospel to bind up our wounds. Not until the law has arrested and imprisoned us will we long for Christ to set us free. Not until the law has condemned and killed us will we call on Christ for justification and life.

Question 5. All parents know the costliness of love and what it means to be torn apart by conflicting emotions, especially when there is a need to punish a child. Perhaps the boldest of all human models of God in Scripture is the pain of parenthood when it is attributed to him in Hosea 11. Forgiveness is for God the Father the profoundest of problems. Sin and wrath stand in the way. God must not only respect us as the responsible beings we are, but he must also respect himself as the holy God he is. The passage bears witness to a struggle between what God ought to do because of his righteousness and what he cannot do because of his love. The way God chooses to forgive sinners and reconcile them to himself must first and foremost be fully consistent with his own character. God must satisfy himself in the way of salvation he devises; he cannot save us by contradicting himself. He is never at odds with himself, however much it may appear to us that he is.

It cannot be emphasized too strongly that God's love is the source, not the consequence, of the atonement. God does not love us because Christ died for us; Christ died for us because God loved us. If it is God's wrath which needed to be propitiated, it is God's love which did the propitiating. If it may be said that the propitiation "changed" God, or that by it he changed himself, let us be clear he did not change from wrath to love, or from enmity to grace, since his character is unchanging. What the propitiation changed was his dealings with us.

In verse 21, then, Paul suddenly breaks in with "But now," to reveal to us how God's judgment and love are reconciled in Christ. Over against the unrighteousness of some and the self-righteousness of others, Paul sets the righteousness of God. Over against God's wrath resting on evildoers, he sets God's grace on sinners who believe. Over against judgment, he sets justification—all "through the redemption that came by Christ Jesus" (v. 24).

Question 6. The law cannot justify sinners because its function is to expose and condemn their sin. The reason the law condemns us is that we break it. The law brings the knowledge of sin, not the forgiveness of sin.

Question 7. The phrase "righteousness from God" stresses the saving initiative that God has taken to give sinners a righteous status in his sight. In Romans 3:22 Paul adds that it "comes through faith in Jesus Christ to all who believe" and is offered to all because it is needed by all.

Question 8. The Greek word translated "sacrifice of atonement" is *hilasterion,* which the KJV renders "propitiation." Because to propitiate somebody means to placate his or her anger, it seems to some Christians an unworthy concept of God to suppose that he gets angry and that his wrath needs to be averted. However, Paul is describing God's solution to the human predicament, which is not only sin but God's wrath on sin (Rom 1:18; 2:5; 3:5). Where there is divine wrath, there is the need to avert it. We should not be shy of using the word *propitiation* in relation to the cross, any more than we should drop the word *wrath* in relation to God.

However, propitiation must be purged of all pagan notions. While evil arouses God's anger, God does not fly off the handle or lose his temper. His wrath is neither capricious nor arbitrary. God is not ever irascible, malicious, spiteful or vindictive. His anger is neither mysterious nor irrational. It is never unpredictable, but always predictable, because it is provoked by evil and by evil alone. God's anger is poles apart from ours. What provokes our anger (injured vanity) never provokes his; what provokes his anger (evil) seldom provokes ours.

Question 9. God left unpunished the sins of former generations (Rom 3:25), letting the nations go their own way and overlooking their ignorance. He did this not because of any injustice on his part or with any thought of condoning evil, but because, in his forbearance, it was his intention in the fullness of time to punish these sins in the death of his Son. This was the only way he could both be just, indeed demonstrate his justice, and simultaneously be the one who justifies those who have faith in Jesus. Both justice (the divine attribute) and justification (the divine activity) would be impossible without the cross.

Study 6. Ransomed by God. Hebrews 9:11-28.

Purpose: To clarify that Christ was God himself, sacrificing himself for sinful humanity.

Question 1. The letter to the Hebrews portrays the sacrifice of Jesus Christ as having perfectly fulfilled the Old Testament "shadows" (Heb 8:5; 10:1). For he sacrificed himself (not animals) once and for all (not repeatedly), thus securing for us not only ceremonial cleansing and restoration to favor in the covenant community but the purification of our consciences and restoration to fellowship with the living God.

Question 3. Christ served as both the high priest who offered the sacrifice and the sacrifice itself.

Question 4. God's mediation is both like and unlike human mediation. Often in human situations both parties are reluctant to reconcile. This is not the case for God. The Father is not unwilling to forgive and the Son is not unwilling to die for us. There is no discord between the Father and Son so the Son does not need to prevail upon, much less coerce, the Father to pardon us. Furthermore, the Father does not victimize or punish the Son. The Father and Son are of one mind and one heart to reconcile us and cannot be set against one another in Christ's atoning work.

Question 6. Jesus told his disciples that "the Son of Man did not come to be served, but to serve, and to give his life as a ransom for many" (Mk 10:45)—literally "to give his life as a ransom instead of many." The Servant would not be served but serve and would complete his service by suffering, specifically by laying down his life as a ransom instead of many. It was only by serving that he would be served, only by suffering that he would enter into his glory.

Questions 7-8. Verses 16-22 refer to Moses' actions after God gave the Ten Commandments (Ex 24:3-8) and during the consecration of the tabernacle priests (Lev 8:14-15, 18-19). Here we find the crucial text "without the shedding of blood there is no forgiveness" (Heb 9:22; see also Lev 17:11). No forgiveness without blood means no atonement without substitution. There has to be life for life or blood for blood.

But the Old Testament blood sacrifices were only shadows; the substance is Christ. For a substitute to be effective, it must be an appropriate equivalent. Animal sacrifices cannot atone for human beings because a human being is "much more valuable . . . than a sheep," as Jesus himself said (Matthew 12:12). And his personal sinlessness uniquely qualified him to bear our sins in our place. Only "the precious blood of Christ" is valuable enough (1 Pet 1:19).

Questions 11-12. We are obliged to conclude that the cross was a substitutionary sacrifice. Christ died for us. Christ died instead of us. He voluntarily accepted liability for our sins. It is the Judge himself who, in holy love, assumed the role of the innocent victim; for in and through the person of his Son, he himself bore the penalty that he himself inflicted. The righteous, loving Father humbled himself to become, in and through his only Son, flesh, sin and a curse for us, in order to redeem us without compromising his own character.

Study 7. Justified. Titus 3:3-8.
Purpose: To examine justification as a scriptural picture of salvation.
Question 1. Group members' answers may vary. Some might focus on Paul's regret over past sins and find it negative (v. 3). Others may focus on our future hope (v. 7) or catch Paul's amazement at how God's love has "appeared" (v. 4). Others may see only overwhelming gratitude. Still others may feel Paul's sense of unworthiness in light of God's undeserved mercy.
Question 2. No matter how participants answered question 1, this question gives them the opportunity to enter into Paul's experience and realize its universality for all Christians.
Question 4. Having established our sinfulness in verse 3, Paul sets forth God's kindness and love, his undeserved mercy in salvation, his cleansing and renewing by the Holy Spirit generously poured out through Christ, our justification by grace, and our hope of eternal life.
Question 5. Standing before the cross we begin to get a clear view both of God and of ourselves, especially in relation to each other. Instead of inflicting on us the judgment we deserve, God in Christ endured it in our place. Hell is the only alternative. This is the scandal, the stumbling block, of the cross. Our proud hearts rebel against it. We cannot bear to acknowledge either the seriousness of our sin and guilt or our utter indebtedness to the cross. Surely, we say, there must be something we can do, or at least contribute, in order to make amends? We cannot stand the humiliation of acknowledging our bankruptcy and allowing somebody else to pay for us. The notion that this somebody else should be God himself is just too much to take. We would rather perish than repent, rather lose ourselves than humble ourselves. Only the Christian gospel demands such an abject self-humbling on our part, for it alone teaches divine substitution as the only way of salvation.
Questions 6-8. *Justification* is not a synonym for *amnesty,* which is strictly pardon without principle, a forgiveness that overlooks—even forgets (*amnestia* is "forgetfulness")—wrongdoing and declines to bring it to justice. No, justification is an act of gracious justice.

When God justifies sinners, he is not declaring bad people to be good or saying that they are not sinners after all; he is pronouncing them legally righteous, free from any liability to the broken law, because he himself, in his Son, bore the penalty of our lawbreaking.

Four of Paul's key phrases summarize his defense of this divine justification of sinners. First, the source of our justification is indicated in the expression "justified by his grace," that is, by his utterly undeserved favor, which occurs in Titus 3:7 and in Romans 3:24. The grounds for our justification are that we are "justified by his blood" (Rom 5:9). There could be no justification without atonement. The means of our justification is indicated in Paul's favorite expression "justified by faith" (Rom 3:28; 5:1 ["justified through faith"]; Gal 2:16; 3:24). Grace and faith belong indissolubly to one another, since faith's only function is to receive what grace freely offers. Fourth, the effects of our justification can be deduced from Paul's expression "justified in Christ" (Gal 2:17), which points to the personal relationship with him that, by faith, we now enjoy.

Question 7. The great affirmation "he saved us" is broken down into its component parts: "the washing of rebirth and renewal by the Holy Spirit" and being "justified by his grace" (vv. 5-7). Regeneration by the Holy Spirit is not an aspect of justification, but both are aspects of salvation, and neither can take place without the other. Once we hold fast that the work of the Son for us and the work of the Spirit in us—justification and regeneration—are inseparable twins, it is safe to go on insisting that justification is an external, legal declaration that the sinner has been put right with God, forgiven and reinstated.

Question 11. The consistent teaching of the New Testament is that salvation leads to grateful obedience to Christ. We obey him out of love for him. Still we must counteract our natural tendency to be lazy and selfish; we need encouragement and incentive to do good. In a similar way Paul urged the Galatian believers, "Let us not become weary in doing good, for at the proper time we will reap a harvest if we do not give up" (Gal 6:9).

Study 8. The Revelation of God. John 1:1-18.

Purpose: To investigate how the cross of Christ reveals God's character.

Question 1. The most straightforward reference is verse 18, which states that God the One and Only "has made him known." All the references to "light" (vv. 4, 7-9) refer to God's revelation, with their clear contrast between light and darkness, between being able to see and not being able to see. Verses 10-13 contrast those who recognize or do not recognize Christ, that is, those who know or do not know him. John boldly states that "we have seen his glory" (v. 14). Group members may discern other references as well.

Question 2. If God had sent a mere human being to us, as he sent the prophets to Israel, we would have been grateful. If he had sent an angel, as he did to Mary at the annunciation, we would have counted it a great privilege. Yet in either case he would have sent us a third party, since people and angels are creatures of his making. But in sending his own Son, eternally begotten from his own Being, he was not sending a creature, a third party, but giving himself, and love is in its essence self-giving.

It's not just the fact that God came to earth, however. It would have been wonderful if God had only given his Son, and so himself, to become flesh and live and give and serve for us on earth. But the incarnation is but the beginning of his self-giving. He gives himself to the uttermost, to the torture of crucifixion and the horror of sin-bearing and God-forsakenness, for us.

Question 3. "Word" in Greek is *logos,* which is "the transliteration of a common Greek word that generally means 'word,' 'speech,' 'account,' 'story' or 'message.'" John's Gospel "uses *logos* in a particular way to refer to Jesus. . . . The Word is the person of the Godhead through whom the world was created, who took on human nature in history and who is the source of life and light for humanity" (David H. Johnson, "Logos," in *Dictionary of Jesus and the Gospels,* ed. Joel B. Green, Scot McKnight and I. Howard Marshall [Downers Grove, Ill.: InterVarsity Press, 1992], pp. 481, 483).

Question 5. To illustrate the contrast between a true light and a false light, it may be helpful to think of the crew of a ship at night watching for a lighthouse. The lighthouse is the true light which will accurately show the way into a safe harbor. Pirates could set up a false light that appears to be the lighthouse but that would lead the sailors into a fatal trap.

Question 6. As a possible follow-up question ask, "Why do you think people have trouble recognizing God in Christ?"

Question 7. God's glory, which overshadowed and filled the tabernacle in the wilderness, was now displayed in him who "lived for a while" (literally tabernacled) among us. As Yahweh showed Moses his glory by declaring his name to be both merciful and righteous (Ex 34:5-7), so the glory we have seen in Jesus Christ was "full of grace and truth."

The self-humiliation of the Son of God, which began in the incarnation, culminated in his death. Yet in that very abasement of himself he was "lifted up," not just physically raised on to the cross, but spiritually exalted before the eyes of the world. The cross which appeared to be "shame" was in fact "glory." The glory that radiates from the cross is that same combination of the divine qualities that God revealed to Moses as mercy and justice, and that we have seen in the Word made flesh as "grace and truth."

Question 9. The death of Jesus on the cross cannot be seen as a demonstration of love in itself, but only if he gave his life in order to rescue ours. His death must be seen to have had an objective before it can have an appeal. The cross can be seen as a proof of God's love only when it is at the same time seen as a proof of his justice. It was precisely in making a just satisfaction for sin that the manifestation of love took place.

Question 11. Evil in the world is often one of the hardest pieces for people to fit with God's love. Why do we see personal tragedies, floods and earthquakes, hunger and poverty? Christianity offers no glib answers to these agonizing questions. But it does offer evidence of God's love, just as historical and objective as the evidence that seems to deny it, and it is in this light that the world's calamities need to be viewed. Although in this world our attention is constantly arrested by the problems of evil and pain, which seem to contradict God's love, we will be wise not to allow it to be deflected from the cross, where God's love has been publicly and visibly manifested.

Study 9. The Conquest of Evil. Colossians 2:6-15.
Purpose: To enter into the victory over evil that Christ accomplished at the cross.
Group discussion. Here's an alternate or additional question: Consider this statement: "In addition to the salvation of sinners and the revelation of God, the cross secured the conquest of evil." What is your response to that?
Question 4. Paul urges the Colossians to continue to live rooted and built up in Christ as they have been taught. His urgent instructions show that he does not assume their continued growth will happen automatically. He warns against dangerous influences which have genuine power to undermine their faith and draw them into false ideas.
Question 5. As the church goes out on its mission, in the power of the Spirit, to preach Christ crucified as Lord and to summon people to repent and believe in him, the conquest of evil is extended. In every true conversion, turning from sin to Christ is a turning from darkness to light, from the power of Satan to God (Acts 26:18), from idols to serve the living and true God (1 Thess 1:9). Every Christian conversion involves a power encounter in which the devil is obligated to relax his hold on somebody's life and the superior power of Christ is demonstrated.

Christians live in the tension between Christ's victory over evil on the cross and his final victory when he will make all things new. Christ is head over everything (Col 2:10), but as Hebrews 2:8-9 states, "At present we do not see everything subject to him. But we see Jesus, who was made a little lower than the angels, now crowned with glory and honor because he suffered death, so that by the grace of God he might taste death for everyone."
Question 6. Circumcision of the heart was referred to as far back as Moses (Deut 10:16). Paul wrote more extensively about the idea in several letters (e.g., Rom 2:25-29). As circumcision was the sign of the former covenant, Christian baptism is the sign of the new covenant in Christ. From the Day of Pentecost the message of the church has been "Repent and be baptized" (Acts 2:38), in obedience to Jesus' commission to make disciples, "baptizing them in the name of the Father and of the Son and of the Holy Spirit" (Mt 28:19).

Question 7. The "written code" can hardly be the law itself, since Paul regarded it as "holy, righteous and good" (Rom 7:12); it must rather refer to the broken law, which was "against us" and "stood opposed to us" with its judgment. The word Paul uses for the "written code" is *cheirographon,* a handwritten certificate of indebtedness. The apostle employs three verbs to describe how God has dealt with our debts. He "canceled" the bond by literally wiping it clean and then "took it away, nailing it to the cross."

Questions 7-8. In verses 13-15, Paul brings together two different aspects of the saving work of Christ's cross: the forgiveness of our sins and the cosmic overthrow of the principalities and powers. He illustrates the freeness and graciousness of God's forgiveness with the ancient custom of canceling debts. God frees us from our bankruptcy only by paying our debts on Christ's cross.

Then Paul moves from the forgiveness of our sins to the conquest of the evil powers using three graphic verbs to portray their defeat. The first means that Christ stripped them either of their weapons and so disarmed them, or of their power and so degraded them. Second, he made a public spectacle of them, exhibiting them as now powerless, and so third, triumphing over them by the cross, which is probably a reference to the procession of captives who celebrated a victory.

Question 10. Many Christians oscillate between two positions. Some are triumphalists who see only the decisive victory of Jesus Christ and overlook the apostolic warnings against the powers of darkness. Others are defeatists who see only the fearsome malice of the devil and overlook the victory, which Christ has already won. The tension is part of the Christian dilemma between the already and the not yet. An overemphasis on the already leads to triumphalism, the claim to perfection, either moral (sinlessness) or physical (complete health), which belongs only to the consummated kingdom, the not yet. An overemphasis on the not yet leads to defeatism, an acquiescence in continuing evil which is incompatible with the already of Christ's victory.

The reality is that though the devil has been defeated, he has not yet conceded defeat. Although he has been overthrown, he has not yet been eliminated. In fact he continues to wield great power. This is the reason for the tension we feel in both our theology and our experience.

Study 10. The Community of Celebration. 1 Peter 2:4-10.

Purpose: To encourage Christians to see ourselves as part of a joyful, redeemed community.

Questions 1-2. Peter describes what is true about Christian believers. He does not necessarily describe how we feel all the time. We are living stones in a spiritual house, a holy and royal priesthood, a holy nation, a people belonging to God.

One note specifically about the people of God as "a holy priesthood" (v. 5) and "a royal priesthood" (v. 9): This is the famous priesthood of all believers on which the Reformers laid great stress. In consequence of this universal priesthood, the word "priest" (Greek *hiereus*) is never in the New Testament applied to the ordained minister. The minister shares in offering what the people offer but has no distinctive offering to make that differs from theirs.

Question 5. Participants may come up with many different examples from their own experience. Eight kinds of spiritual sacrifices are mentioned in Scripture. First, we are to present our bodies to him for his service, as "living sacrifices" (Rom 12:1); that sounds like a material offering, but it is termed "spiritual worship," presumably because it pleases God only if it expresses the worship of the heart. Second, we offer God our praise, worship and thanksgiving, "the fruit of lips that confess his name" (Heb 13:15). Our third sacrifice is prayer, which is said to ascend to God like fragrant incense (Rev 5:8). Our fourth is "a broken and contrite heart," which God accepts and never despises (Ps 51:17). Fifth, faith is called a "sacrifice and service" (Phil 2:17). Sixth are our gifts and good deeds, "for with such sacrifices God is pleased" (Heb 13:16). The seventh sacrifice is our life "poured out like a drink offering" in God's service, even unto death (2 Tim 4:6). The eighth is the special offering of the evangelist, whose preaching of the gospel is called a "priestly duty" because the evangelist's converts can be presented as "an offering acceptable to God" (Rom 15:16).

Question 6. Verse 6 quotes Isaiah 28:16, which is in the context of God's promise that evil will be found out, judged and swept away. The person who trusts in the Lord will endure and will not be touched by the judgment. Verse 7 quotes Psalm 118:22; the psalmist's next words confirm that the Lord is the one who put the stone in place: "The Lord has done this, / and it is marvelous in our eyes" (Ps 118:23). Verse 8 quotes Isaiah 8:14, which also calls the Lord a sanctuary for those who trust him while promising that unfaithful Israel will "fall and be broken" (Is 8:15).

Question 8. The brief time we spend together on the Lord's day, far from being divorced from the rest of our lives, is intended to bring our lives into sharp focus. Humbly (as sinners) yet boldly (as forgiven sinners) we press into God's presence, responding to his loving initiative with an answering love of our own, worshiping him with musical instruments and articulating our joy in songs of praise. Singing is a unique feature of Christian worship. Whenever Christian people come together it is impossible to keep them from singing. The Christian community is a community of celebration.

Question 9. As possible follow-up questions, ask: "When you enter into worship with other Christians, are you aware of gratitude to God in your own heart? Do others encourage you to be thankful? Do you encourage others to be thankful?"

Question 11. The community of Christ is the community of the cross. Having been brought into being by the cross, it continues to live by and under the cross. Our perspective and our behavior are now governed by the cross. All our relationships have been radically transformed by it. The cross is not just a badge to identify us and the banner under which we march; it is also the compass that gives us our bearings in a disoriented world.

Study 11. Self-Understanding and Self-Giving. Luke 9:23-27; 12:22-34.

Purpose: To reach a true understanding of ourselves in light of the cross.

Questions 1-2. Our self is not a simple entity that is either wholly good or wholly evil; therefore it is neither to be totally valued nor totally denied. What we are (our self or personal identity) is partly the result of the creation (the image of God) and partly the result of the Fall (the image defaced). The self we are to deny, disown and crucify is our fallen self, everything within us that's incompatible with Jesus Christ. The self we are to affirm and value is our created self, everything within us that's compatible with Jesus Christ.

The cross is the God-given measure of the value of our true self, since Christ loved us and died for us. On the other hand, it is the God-given model for the denial of our false self, since we are to nail it to the cross and so put it to death. Or, more simply, standing before the cross we see simultaneously our worth and our unworthiness, since we perceive both the greatness of his love in dying, and the greatness of our sin in causing him to die.

Question 3. Allow any and all reactions to Jesus' words. Some participants may embrace what Jesus says here, while others may be unsettled or even frightened by his words. Acknowledge that Jesus calls us to a radical kind of self-abandonment, but he promises that this is how we will find authentic life.

Question 4. We usually interpret the command to deny ourselves to mean "deny ourselves something," such as a favorite food or a cherished pastime. Jesus calls us to something more basic, more difficult and ultimately more satisfying: to renounce our selves, our own selfish demand to run our own lives. To deny ourselves is to behave toward ourselves as Peter did toward Jesus when he denied him three times. The verb is the same (*aparneomai*). He disowned him, repudiated him, turned his back on him.

Question 5. If we are following Jesus with a cross on our shoulder, there is only one place we are going: the place of crucifixion. Our cross is not an illness or an irritable family member; it is the symbol of death to self.

Question 6. True self-denial (the denial of our false, fallen self) is not the road to self-destruction but the road to self-discovery.

Study 12. Loving Our Enemies. Romans 12:9; 12:14—13:5.

Purpose: To develop a Christian attitude toward evil, especially toward those who personally oppose us.

Question 1. These verses define what our Christian attitude to evil should be. First, evil is to be hated (v. 9). Whenever love is "sincere," literally without hypocrisy, it is morally discerning. It never pretends that evil is anything else, nor does it condone evil. Second, evil is not to be repaid (vv. 17, 19). Revenge and retaliation are absolutely forbidden to the people of God. To repay evil for evil is to add one evil to another. Third, evil is to be overcome (vv. 14, 18, 20-21). In the new community of Jesus, curses are to be replaced by blessings, malice by prayer, and revenge by service. Fourth, evil is to be punished. The fourth point will be dealt with in the second portion of Scripture, Romans 13:1-5.

Question 2. Paul wrote his letter to the Romans in about A.D. 57. Nero was emperor in Rome. Although Nero had not yet begun his intense persecution of Christians, there was inevitable conflict between pagan emperor-worship and Christian worship of the Son of God. By referring to "the one in authority" as "God's servant to do you good" (Rom 3:3-4), Paul acknowledges the sovereignty of God over all worldly forces. Christians not only in Rome but throughout the Roman Empire needed to have a firm grasp on the fact that God is able to bring about good and work his will even through pagan rulers.

Question 3. It may seem strange that the exhortation to love is followed immediately by a command to hate (v. 9). But love is not the blind sentiment it is traditionally said to be. On the contrary, love is discerning. It is so passionately devoted to the beloved that it hates every evil that is incompatible with his or her highest welfare. Both verbs in verse 9 are strong, almost vehement. Love's hatred of evil expresses an aversion, an abhorrence, even a loathing, while love's clinging to what is good expresses a sticking or bonding as if with glue. Compromise with evil is incompatible with love. God hates evil because his love is holy love; we must hate it too.

Questions 5-6. The Christian ethic is never purely negative. Each of Paul's four negative imperatives is accompanied by a positive counterpart. We are not to curse but to bless (v. 14); we are not to retaliate but to do what is right and live at peace (vv. 17-18); we are not to take revenge but to leave this to God, and meanwhile to serve our enemies (vv. 19-20); and we are not to be overcome by evil, but to overcome evil with good (v. 21).

A note on verse 20: To "heap burning coals" on an enemy's head sounds like an unfriendly act, incompatible with loving your enemy. But it is a figure of speech for causing an acute sense of shame, not in order to hurt or humiliate an enemy but in order to bring the person to repentance, and so to overcome evil with good.

Question 7. The Christian attitude toward the state should be one of critical respect. The origin of the state's authority is God (vv. 1-2). It is extremely impressive that Paul writes not only of the state's authority but of ministry too. The one in authority is "God's servant" (v. 4). In spite of the defects of Roman government, with which Paul was personally familiar, he emphatically declared its authority and ministry to be God's. The state must be respected as a divine institution; but to give it our blind, unqualified allegiance would be idolatry.

Question 8. The phrase "to do you good" (v. 4) is not explained, but it surely covers all the social benefits of good government, preserving the peace, maintaining law and order, protecting human rights, promoting justice and caring for the needy. On the other hand, the state, as the minister of God and agent of his wrath, punishes wrongdoers, bringing them to justice. Thus, the purpose for which God has given authority to the state is in order both to reward (and so promote) good and to punish (and so restrain) evil. The restraint and punishment of evil are universally recognized as primary responsibilities of the state.

Question 9. The prohibitions at the end of Romans 12 do not mean that evil should be left unrequited pending the day of judgment, but that the punishment should be administered by the state (as the agent of God's wrath) and that it is inappropriate for ordinary citizens to take the law into their own hands.

Group members may raise the logical question of how Christians are to respond when the state is obviously unjust. What if we feel that the people in power are overtly evil? What if we are invaded by forces which want to wipe out Christianity? Christian convictions on the question have varied and continue to vary. Some believers hold to pacifism and refuse to bear arms. Others see volunteering for military combat as a moral duty. For more information, you could look at resources that discuss the concepts of just war and unjust war, such as *War: Four Christian Views*, edited by Robert Clouse (Winona Lake, Ind.: BMH Books, 1991).

Study 13. Suffering and Glory. Hebrews 4:14-16; 5:7-9.

Purpose: To see in Jesus the God who suffers for us and with us.

General note. "Therefore" (4:14) grows from the writer's discussion of the believers' "rest" from our own works.

Question 4. Jesus was never imperfect in the sense that he had done wrong, for Hebrews underlines his sinlessness (Heb 4:15; 7:26). It was rather that he needed further experiences and opportunities in order to become *teleios,* "mature." In particular, he "learned obedience from what he suffered." He was never disobedient to the Father. But his sufferings were the testing-ground in which his obedience became full-grown.

If suffering was the means by which the sinless Christ became mature, then we, in our sinfulness, need it so much more. Just as suffering led to maturity through obedience for Christ, so it leads to maturity through perseverance for us.

Question 6. This is not the place for group members to compare one person's degree of suffering with that of another person. What may seem like a trivial problem to one person may be a painful trial to another. What may be unattractive or even repulsive to one person may be an overpowering temptation to sin for another. The point is for each person to evaluate the effects of his or her own suffering.

Question 7. It is the hope of glory that makes suffering bearable. The essential perspective to develop is that of the eternal purpose of God, which is to make us holy or Christlike. The future prospect that makes suffering endurable is the only reward of priceless value, namely, the glory of Christ, his own image perfectly re-created in us. "We shall be like him, for we shall see him as he is" (1 Jn 3:2).

Scripture also reveals many examples of the results suffering can bring about in us. It fosters perseverance, purifies faith and develops humility, as when Paul's thorn in the flesh keeps him from becoming conceited (2 Cor 12:7). And it deepens insight (for example, through the pain of Hosea's unrequited love for Gomer, the faithfulness of God's love for Israel was revealed to him).

Question 8. There is always an indefinable something about people who have suffered. They have a fragrance that others lack. They exhibit the meekness and gentleness of Christ. Perhaps the real test of our hunger for holiness is our willingness to experience any degree of suffering if God will use it to make us holy.

Question 9. The cross of Christ is the proof of God's personal, loving solidarity with us in our pain. For the real sting of suffering is not misfortune itself, nor even the pain of it or the injustice of it, but the apparent Godforsakenness of it. Pain is endurable, but the seeming indifference of God is not. Sometimes we picture him lounging in some celestial deck-chair while the hungry millions starve to death. It is this terrible caricature of God that the cross smashes to smithereens. We are not to envisage God on a deck-chair but on a cross. The God who allows us to suffer once suffered himself in Christ, and continues to suffer with us and for us today.

The cross does not solve the problem of suffering, but it supplies the essential perspective from which to look at it. Since God has demonstrated his holy love and loving justice in a historical event (the cross), no other historical event (whether personal or global) can override or disprove it.

John Stott is known worldwide as a preacher, evangelist and communicator of Scripture. Stott has written many books, including Basic Christianity *and* Basic Christian Leadership. *This study guide is based on his book* The Cross of Christ.

What Should We Study Next?

A good place to continue your study of Scripture would be with a book study. Many groups begin with a Gospel such as *Mark* (20 studies by Jim Hoover) or *John* (26 studies by Douglas Connelly). These guides are divided into two parts so that if twenty or twenty-six weeks seems like too much to do at once, the group can feel free to do half and take a break with another topic. Later you might want to come back to it. You might prefer to try a shorter letter. *Philippians* (9 studies by Donald Baker), *Ephesians* (11 studies by Andrew T. and Phyllis J. Le Peau) and *1 & 2 Timothy and Titus* (11 studies by Pete Sommer) are good options. If you want to vary your reading with an Old Testament book, consider *Ecclesiastes* (12 studies by Bill and Teresa Syrios) for a challenging and exciting study.

There are a number of interesting topical LifeGuide studies as well. Here are some options for filling three or four quarters of a year:

Basic Discipleship
Christian Beliefs, 12 studies by Stephen D. Eyre
Christian Character, 12 studies by Andrea Sterk & Peter Scazzero
Christian Disciplines, 12 studies by Andrea Sterk & Peter Scazzero
Evangelism, 12 studies by Rebecca Pippert & Ruth Siemens

Building Community
Fruit of the Spirit, 9 studies by Hazel Offner
Spiritual Gifts, 8 studies by R. Paul Stevens
Christian Community, 10 studies by Rob Suggs

Character Studies
David, 12 studies by Jack Kuhatschek
New Testament Characters, 10 studies by Carolyn Nystrom
Old Testament Characters, 12 studies by Peter Scazzero
Women of the Old Testament, 12 studies by Gladys Hunt

The Trinity
Meeting God, 12 studies by J. I. Packer
Meeting Jesus, 13 studies by Leighton Ford
Meeting the Spirit, 10 studies by Douglas Connelly